CRO

For Brandon, who has added three Native American bloods to the Stemple family
–J. Y. and H. E. Y. S.

To Beverly and Howard Friedman, with love and gratitude
–R. R.

ACKNOWLEDGMENTS

With thanks to Angela Brickhouse Minton, Elizabeth Evans, Carl Curnutte III, and Court Watson at *The Lost Colony Symphonic Outdoor Drama;* John Mintz, North Carolina Office of State Archaeology; Charles R. Ewen, Ph.D., Associate Professor of Anthropology, East Carolina University; and Joseph Bruchac, who helped us with the Native American issues.

ISBN-13: 978-0-439-02452-5
ISBN-10: 0-439-02452-8

12 11 10 9 8 7 6 5 4 8 9 10 11 12/0

Printed in the U.S.A. 40

First Scholastic printing, January 2007

Book design by Paul Zakris and Mark Siegel

The text of this book is set in 14-point Minister Book.

A NOTE FROM THE ARTIST

The illustrations in this book were done in a series of stages. First I did tiny, rough "thumbnail" sketches. This is really the fun and creative part for me. Then from these thumbnails I made large, detailed pencil drawings, which I traced onto watercolor paper. Next I painted the pictures using transparent watercolors, adding pencil for detail and texture.

BIBLIOGRAPHY

BOOKS AND ARTICLES

Aron, Paul. *The Unsolved Mysteries of American History.* New York: John Wiley and Sons, 1997.

Brogan, Hugh. *The Penguin History of the United States of America.* New York: Penguin Books, 1985.

Dial, Adolph L. *The Lumbee.* New York: Chelsea House Publishers, 1993.

Houston, Lebame, and Barbara Hird. "John White, Artist and Actor in the Colony." Roanoke Colony souvenir program, Roanoke Island Historical Association (1999): 14-16.

—, eds. *Roanoke Revisited: The Story of the Lost Colony—A Modernized Version of Original Documents.* Manteo, N.C.: Times Printing Company, 1997.

King, J. C. H. *First Peoples, First Contacts.* Cambridge, Mass.: Harvard University Press, 1999.

Kupperman, Karen Ordahl. *Roanoke: The Abandoned Colony.* Savage, Md.: Rowman and Littlefield Publishers, 1984.

Quinn, David Beers. *The Lost Colonists: Their Fortune and Probable Fate.* Raleigh: The North Carolina Division of Archives and History, 1984.

"Roanoke Island: The First English Colonies in America." Roanoke Colony souvenir program, Roanoke Island Historical Association (1998): 7-8.

Waldman, Carl. *Encyclopedia of Native American Tribes.* New York: Checkmark Books, 1999.

WEB SITES

"Forts of the Roanoke Voyages, 1584–1590" (http://www.nps.gov/fora/forts.htm)

"John White" (http://www.nps.gov/fora/jwhite.htm)

"Ships of the Roanoke Voyages" (http://www.nps.gov/fora/shipsdoc.htm)

"Theories: Which One Do You Think Is True?" (http://tqjunior.advanced.org/3826/page3.html)

"The White Doe Inn" (http://whitedoeinn.com/)

"Virginia Indians: The Powhatans, The People" (http://falcon.jmu.edu/~ramseyil/vaindianspowpeople.htm)

ROANOKE
The Lost Colony

AN UNSOLVED MYSTERY FROM HISTORY

BY JANE YOLEN AND HEIDI ELISABET YOLEN STEMPLE

ILLUSTRATED BY ROGER ROTH

SCHOLASTIC INC.

New York Toronto London Auckland Sydney
Mexico City New Delhi Hong Kong Buenos Aires

N
W
E
S

When I grow up I want to be a detective, just like my dad. He says I was born curious, and curiosity is the best tool a detective can have.

Right now I'm curious about old mysteries that have never been solved. In police terms these cases are called "open," but Dad and I call them "unsolved mysteries from history," and I am determined to figure out at least one of them.

For each mystery I collect as much about the case as I can. As I go along, I organize the clues in my notebook. Sometimes I use time lines. And I always keep a list of words that are important to the case.

Roanoke: The Lost Colony is about a group of English people who came to the American continent in the 1500s to begin a new settlement. They all disappeared. Though lots of people have ideas—or theories—about what might have happened, no one is sure. My dad says no mystery is impossible to solve as long as you have enough clues.

This is how the story goes.

The word *Roanoke* comes from the Roanoke people, an Algonquin tribe that lived in the area. However, the European settlers who felt they had "discovered" the New World (which consisted of North and South America) also believed they were the land's rightful owners. Without regard for the natives' rights to the land, they considered it part of Virginia and claimed it for their own. Today that piece of coastline is part of North Carolina.

In the year 1587, England and Spain were at war.
A major battleground was the New World.
Along the east coast, forts were scattered,
the one at Roanoke manned by English soldiers.
An early colony of 108 men,
complaining about the harsh conditions
and lack of supplies, had returned home.
They had been poorly prepared
for life in the New World
and had depended upon the native people
for food while treating them badly.
There had been frequent fights and the colonists
had accidentally infected the native people
with European diseases.
A native chief had been slaughtered.
This was not a good way to begin a new settlement.
New soldiers had arrived at the abandoned fort
to hold it until new colonists could arrive.
And colonists were sure to come—
the lure of gold and farmland were too strong
for any complaints to matter.

COLONY/COLONISTS: a group of settlers in a new country, still subjects of their mother country

CHARTER: a royal or government document granting rights

COMMUNITY: a group of people living in one place

John White's drawings recorded everything he saw in the New World. White was not a great artist; in one of his paintings a native woman even had two right feet. His work was to serve science, not art. Only some of John White's paintings survived, about seventy-five originals.

John White was a loyal Englishman and an artist.
He was chosen to lead the colony
by Sir Walter Raleigh, who had been given
the charter to the land in Roanoke by the queen.
White may not have had leadership skills,
but he had already been to the New World.
He had brought back paintings
of the new plants, animals, people.
The colonists were chosen by Raleigh and White
to build the new community.
There were more than sixty men:
farmers, craftsmen, assistants.
There were close to twenty women,
including White's own pregnant daughter,
to work in the fields and houses.
There were almost a dozen children.

The word *Indian* was used for the native people of the New World because Christopher Columbus, landing in the Bahamas, in 1492, thought he was in India. When the colonists landed on Roanoke Island, they referred to the native people as "savages," because they did not understand their customs, manner of dress, or culture. Today "Native American," "Native People," and "Indian" are all acceptable, though the Native Peoples themselves prefer to be known by their individual tribal names.

Two native men were also part of White's group.
One of them, Manteo, had traveled
in the company of the English before.
John White hoped they would help the colonists
with the local native people.
He knew that the earlier colonists had had problems
with fights, with diseases, with killings,
though he had never told Raleigh.
He was sure that with the soldiers already at the fort
and with Manteo to help,
he could keep his colonists safe.

For long ocean journeys several types of ships were generally used, including:

Flagship—the fleet's largest, best, or safest ship, on which the commander sailed

Flyboat—a large boat with one or two masts, generally square rigged

Pinnace—a smaller, faster, more maneuverable boat that sometimes carried oars

FERTILE: capable of supporting a plentiful crop

TORTOISE: land turtle of the warm climates; a good food source because the meat doesn't spoil quickly

The colonists left Portsmouth on April 26, 1587.
They planned to meet with the soldiers,
then go to Chesapeake Bay, north of Roanoke,
where the land was more fertile and the harbor was safer.
They sailed in three boats: a flyboat; a pinnace;
and the flagship, *Lyon*.
After a month and a half at sea
they reached the Americas at last,
stopping first on several islands.
At Santa Cruz several colonists ate green fruit.
Their lips and tongues swelled badly.
A number of people drank from a pond
that had "water so evil" they fell dreadfully ill.
Some who washed their faces in the water
had swollen eyes for five or six days after.
They captured five huge tortoises for meat—
so large, sixteen men became exhausted
hauling them back to the ship.

At last the flagship dropped anchor
outside Roanoke's shallow harbor.
White and forty of his men
planned to take the pinnace to shore
to meet with the soldiers,
then continue on to Chesapeake
where they were going to stay.
But the ship's pilot, Simon Fernandez, had other ideas.
He refused to take the colonists any farther
and put them all ashore at Roanoke.
When White and his men got to the fort
ahead of the larger group of colonists,
they found it razed.
Great melon vines grew in what remained of the houses.
Deer grazed there.
All that was left of the soldiers was a single skeleton.
"We must make the best of what we have," said White,
so they began to repair the houses.

RAZED: destroyed completely
by having been torn down

The coastline that the colonists sailed along is made up of dangerous inlets and coves. A ship coming upon the shore first encounters barrier islands parallel to the coastline, then the mainland itself. At the bottom of these waters—sometimes called the "Graveyard of the Atlantic"—hundreds of ships and boats lie wrecked.

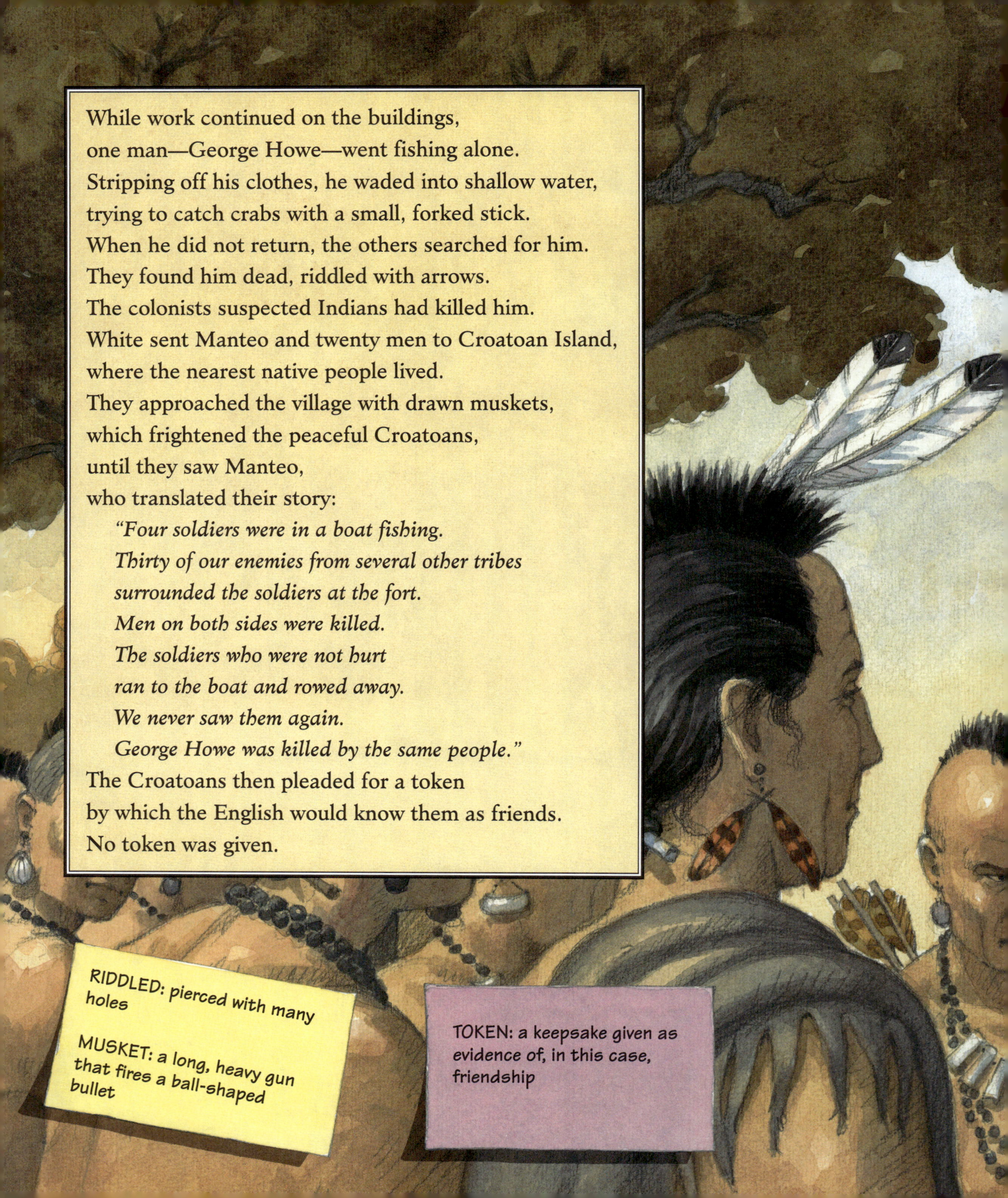

While work continued on the buildings,
one man—George Howe—went fishing alone.
Stripping off his clothes, he waded into shallow water,
trying to catch crabs with a small, forked stick.
When he did not return, the others searched for him.
They found him dead, riddled with arrows.
The colonists suspected Indians had killed him.
White sent Manteo and twenty men to Croatoan Island,
where the nearest native people lived.
They approached the village with drawn muskets,
which frightened the peaceful Croatoans,
until they saw Manteo,
who translated their story:

"Four soldiers were in a boat fishing.
Thirty of our enemies from several other tribes
surrounded the soldiers at the fort.
Men on both sides were killed.
The soldiers who were not hurt
ran to the boat and rowed away.
We never saw them again.
George Howe was killed by the same people."

The Croatoans then pleaded for a token
by which the English would know them as friends.
No token was given.

RIDDLED: pierced with many holes

MUSKET: a long, heavy gun that fires a ball-shaped bullet

TOKEN: a keepsake given as evidence of, in this case, friendship

One Indian—a man named Wanchese, who had himself visited England and was known by the soldiers—was part of a plot to starve the soldiers out. Later he led his people against the colonists, killing George Howe.

Later that week the English mounted
a surprise attack in the middle of the night
on the people they thought had killed Howe.
Spying a campfire, they shot one man
and chased the others through the reeds—
including women and children.
But the colonists had made a terrible mistake.
These were the friendly Croatoans,
who—knowing their enemies had left the area—
had come to gather up peas, corn, pumpkin, tobacco.
As a reward for faithful service, the English
christened Manteo a few days later,
calling him Lord of Roanoke and Dasemunkepeuc.
They thought that this would make him
a better friend to the English
and a loyal subject of Queen Elizabeth.
What Manteo thought of the ceremony is unknown.

A christening is a ceremony in which an individual is admitted into the Christian Church by baptism. During this ceremony a name can be given to a child, or a title to an older individual.

PLIGHT: a difficult and serious situation

DESTINATION: a place to which someone is going

White buried his most prized possessions because other times when he'd left for several days on scouting or drawing trips, many of his supplies had been used by others. He was taking no chances.

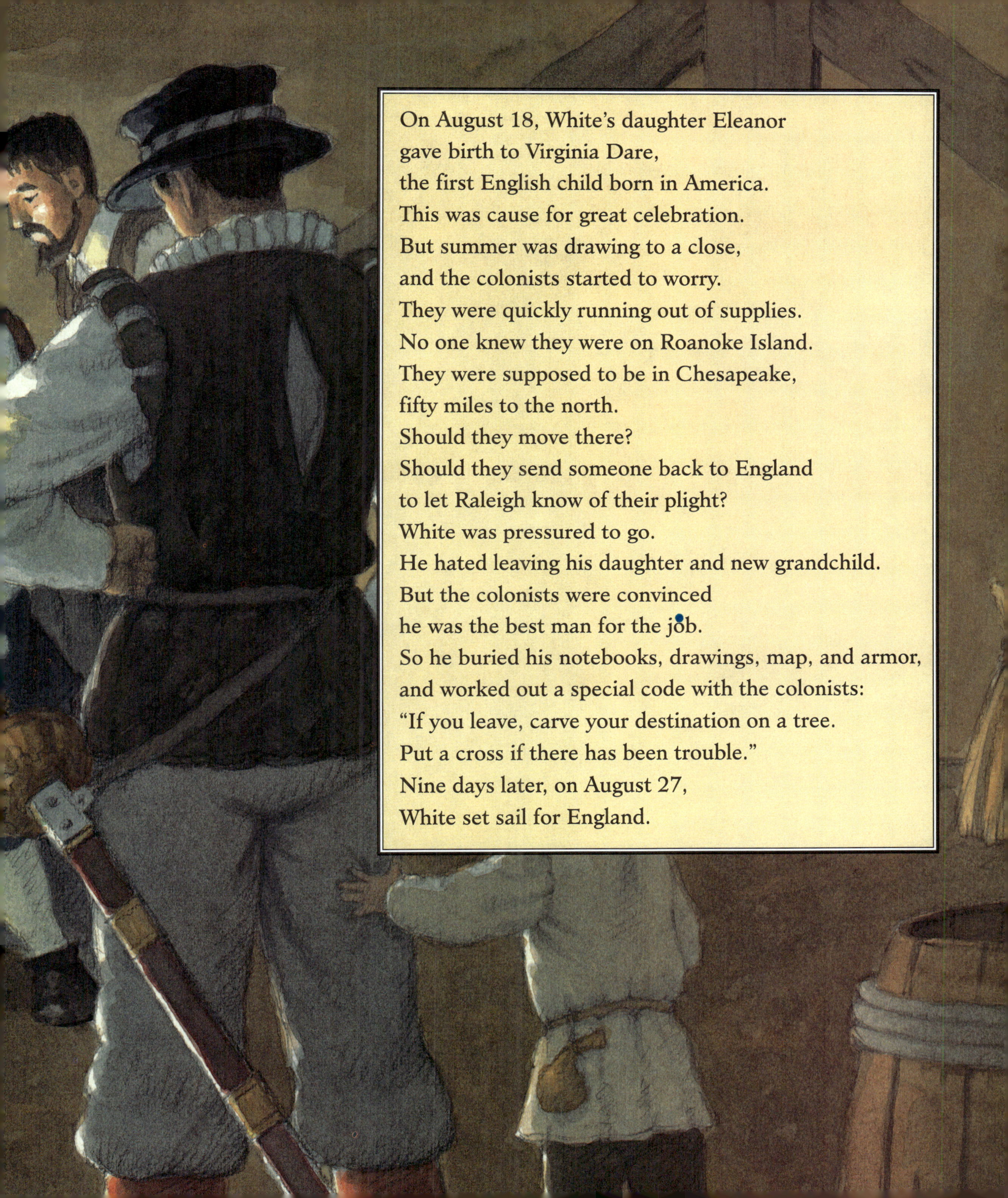

On August 18, White's daughter Eleanor
gave birth to Virginia Dare,
the first English child born in America.
This was cause for great celebration.
But summer was drawing to a close,
and the colonists started to worry.
They were quickly running out of supplies.
No one knew they were on Roanoke Island.
They were supposed to be in Chesapeake,
fifty miles to the north.
Should they move there?
Should they send someone back to England
to let Raleigh know of their plight?
White was pressured to go.
He hated leaving his daughter and new grandchild.
But the colonists were convinced
he was the best man for the job.
So he buried his notebooks, drawings, map, and armor,
and worked out a special code with the colonists:
"If you leave, carve your destination on a tree.
Put a cross if there has been trouble."
Nine days later, on August 27,
White set sail for England.

The Spanish Armada was a fleet of 130 heavy galleons, or warships, and 30,000 men. It was thought to be unbeatable. Spain tried to invade England in 1588. But the English ships were smaller, faster, and easier to maneuver in the channel between England and the European continent. Plus, England had control of all the ports. The armada was eventually crushed entirely by the English.

CONSPIRED: combined into a common effort

PRIVATEERING: acting legally as a pirate with a letter of commission from the king or queen

White left Roanoke in a storm, an awful crossing,
desperate to get to England, desperate to round up
supplies, desperate to return quickly to Roanoke Colony.
But politics, war, and the Spanish Armada
all conspired to keep him in England.
There was nothing he could do.
Half a year later, in the spring, White tried to sail
with two small ships filled with sailors,
fifteen new colonists, and supplies.
But the sailors insisted on privateering along the way.
They attacked not only Spanish ships,
but a Scottish boat and a French ship as well.
White was wounded twice in hand-to-hand combat.
All of the colonists' supplies were stolen.
They limped back to England.

It was March 20, 1590,
before Raleigh could gather enough money
to send any other ships.
Five months later,
having survived storms and more fights,
the ships anchored at the tip of Croatoan Island.
Finally they moved on to the outer islands.
Even though it was evening,
White and his men could see smoke rising
from the vicinity of the Roanoke fort.
In the morning they tried to row ashore
in two small boats through terrible waves.
One boat capsized.
Seven men drowned.

VICINITY: the surrounding area

CROAT

Anchoring in the shallow harbor that night,
they tried to alert the colonists
by sounding a trumpet,
by singing English folk songs loudly,
by calling out to the people on shore.
There was no answer.
In the morning they went to the fort.
It was completely empty.
Carved into a tree near the village
were the letters CRO.
On one of the palisade posts
was the word CROATOAN.
There was no cross indicating any trouble.
All that they found inside the fort
were bars of iron, pigs of lead, iron shot.
Once-buried chests lay overturned, ransacked,
including White's own possessions.
The pinnace used by the colonists was gone.
Weeds grew everywhere.

PALISADE: a high fence with large posts set firmly in the ground
PIGS: oblong masses of a particular kind of metal—in this case, lead
IRON SHOT: pellets of iron that are shot from a gun

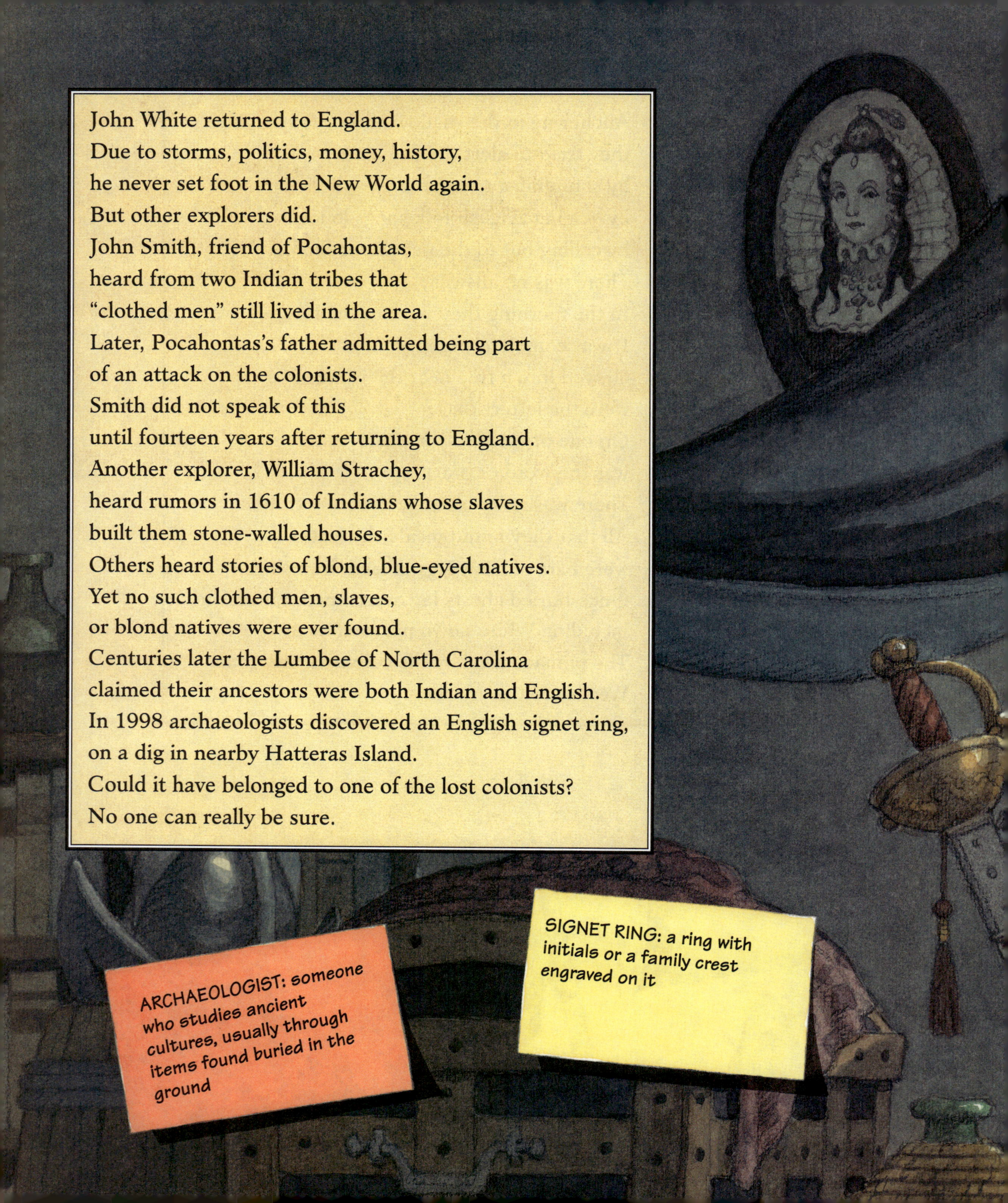

John White returned to England.
Due to storms, politics, money, history,
he never set foot in the New World again.
But other explorers did.
John Smith, friend of Pocahontas,
heard from two Indian tribes that
"clothed men" still lived in the area.
Later, Pocahontas's father admitted being part
of an attack on the colonists.
Smith did not speak of this
until fourteen years after returning to England.
Another explorer, William Strachey,
heard rumors in 1610 of Indians whose slaves
built them stone-walled houses.
Others heard stories of blond, blue-eyed natives.
Yet no such clothed men, slaves,
or blond natives were ever found.
Centuries later the Lumbee of North Carolina
claimed their ancestors were both Indian and English.
In 1998 archaeologists discovered an English signet ring,
on a dig in nearby Hatteras Island.
Could it have belonged to one of the lost colonists?
No one can really be sure.

ARCHAEOLOGIST: someone who studies ancient cultures, usually through items found buried in the ground

SIGNET RING: a ring with initials or a family crest engraved on it

The Lumbee people are a tribe who live primarily in and around Robeson County, which is inland in North Carolina, just above the South Carolina border. They are convinced that the colonists from Roanoke married into the tribe. In fact, a number of them have the same last name as some of the Roanoke settlers.

So what really happened?

According to my dad, no one knows for sure.

But now you have the whole story. You have studied my notes, the time line, and the word lists. Perhaps you can solve the mystery of the Roanoke Colony. Maybe you'll believe one of the old theories of what happened. Or maybe you'll come up with a theory of your own.

Only remember, as my dad always says, *Check your clues.*

1. The No Survivors Theory:

The colonists of Roanoke Colony were killed by the local native people, bent on revenge, or by the Spanish explorers who also wanted to colonize the same area.

Did either group have reason for killing the colonists?

Was there any evidence of murder?

Was there any sign of distress such as an engraved cross?

2. Absorbed by Native People Theory:

The colonists lived with the native people and eventually became part of the tribes by either marrying into the group or being captured as slaves.

What would have made the colonists leave their homes?

Was there any evidence of fighting?

Did the native people keep slaves and were any European slaves ever sighted or found?

Do the Lumbee people claim to have European ancestors?

3. The Lost at Sea Theory:

The colonists tried to sail home to England and got lost at sea.

Could the pinnace have carried a hundred colonists?

Could it have gotten through Spanish blockades or fought a major battle?

Could it have survived major storms?

Did the colonists leave clues as to where they were going?

Did they bring their weapons and possessions?

4. The Split Community Theory:

The majority of the Roanoke colonists took the boat and sailed north as planned to Chesapeake, leaving behind a small contingent at the fort. The smaller group eventually left to go to Croatoan Island.

What clues were left behind?

Were any of the colonists ever found at either Croatoan Island or Chesapeake?

What would have made them split up?

5. The White Doe Theory:

There is a legend that Virginia Dare was raised by the Croatoan people, and when she refused to marry an old medicine man who loved her, he turned her into a white deer.

Even today people claim to see a mysterious white deer bounding through the North Carolina forests.

Is there credible evidence of shape-shifting spells?

Why would the local native people tell stories about Virginia Dare?

1492
Christopher Columbus first arrives in what is now North America

1513
Ponce de Leon claims Florida for Spain

1585
Fort built at Roanoke

1586
Colonists return to England
Soldiers arrive and stay to hold the fort

1587
John White & his colonists set up colony at Roanoke

1588
Spanish look for Roanoke, find no one

1590
John White finally returns to Roanoke, finds no one, returns to England

1607
John Smith hears stories of colonists

1776
Declaration of Independence is signed

1587

April 26	John White and the colonists leave Portsmouth, England
May 8	Colonists set sail for Virginia
June 22	Colonists land at Santa Cruz
June 27	Colonists land at Cotesa Island (near Puerto Rico)
July 1	Colonists land at Mosquito Bay
July 22	Colonists arrive, intending to meet with soldiers
	John White rows with men to fort
July 25	Colonists join White at fort
July 28	George Howe killed
July 30	Colonists visit native people
August 9	Colonists mistakenly attack and kill friendly natives
August 13	Manteo christened
August 18	Virginia Dare born
August 27	John White leaves for England
October 16	John White arrives in Ireland

These are the five most popular explanations ever given. Are any of them right?

Nobody knows for sure. Not the police, not the lawyers, not the reporters, not the historians, and not even my dad. It is a mystery still waiting to be solved. It is, as my dad says, an open file.

But I've got my own theory about what happened to the lost colony of Roanoke.

And maybe—now—you do too.